I0485285

MANDALAS Coloring Book

For

Mothers

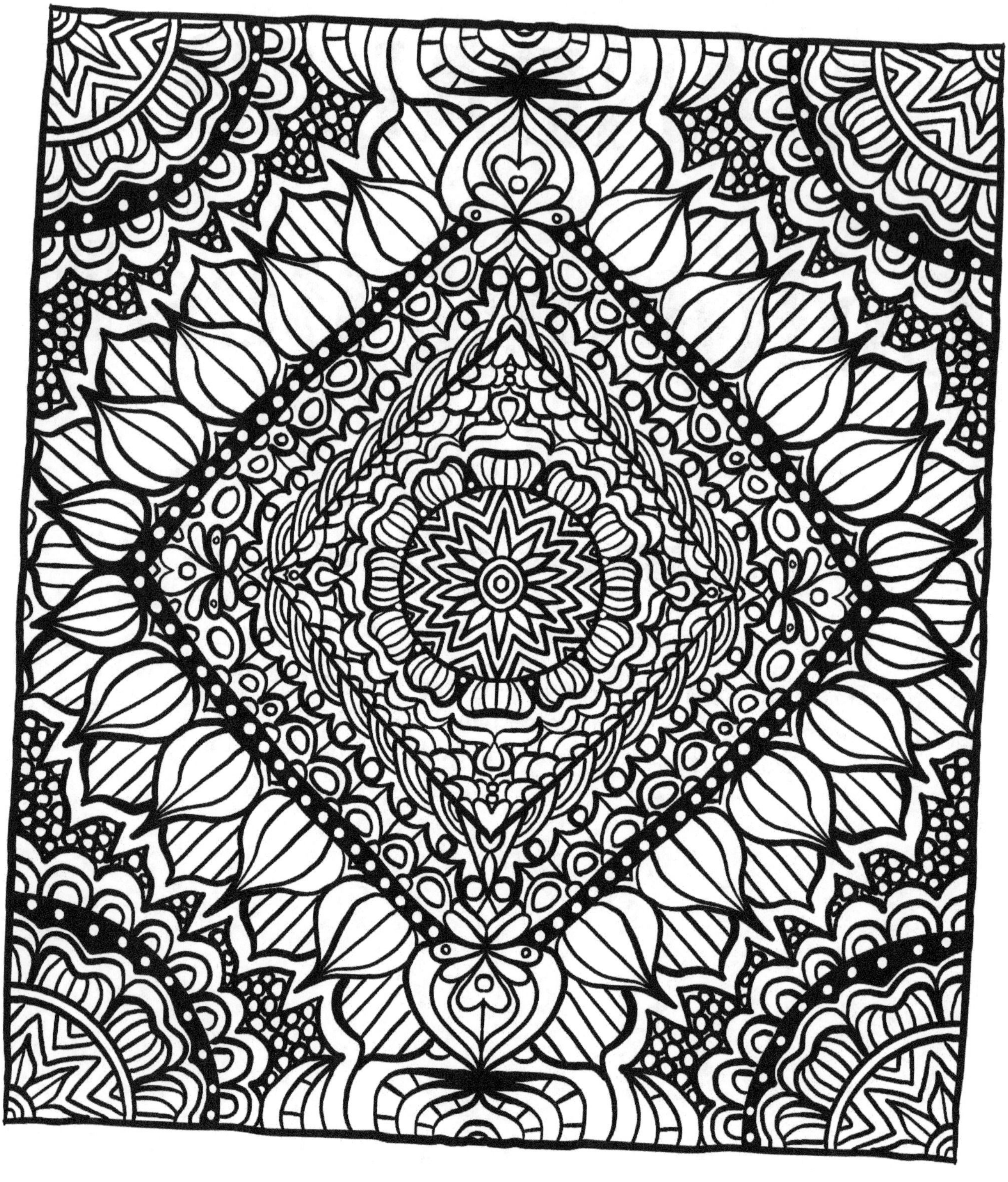

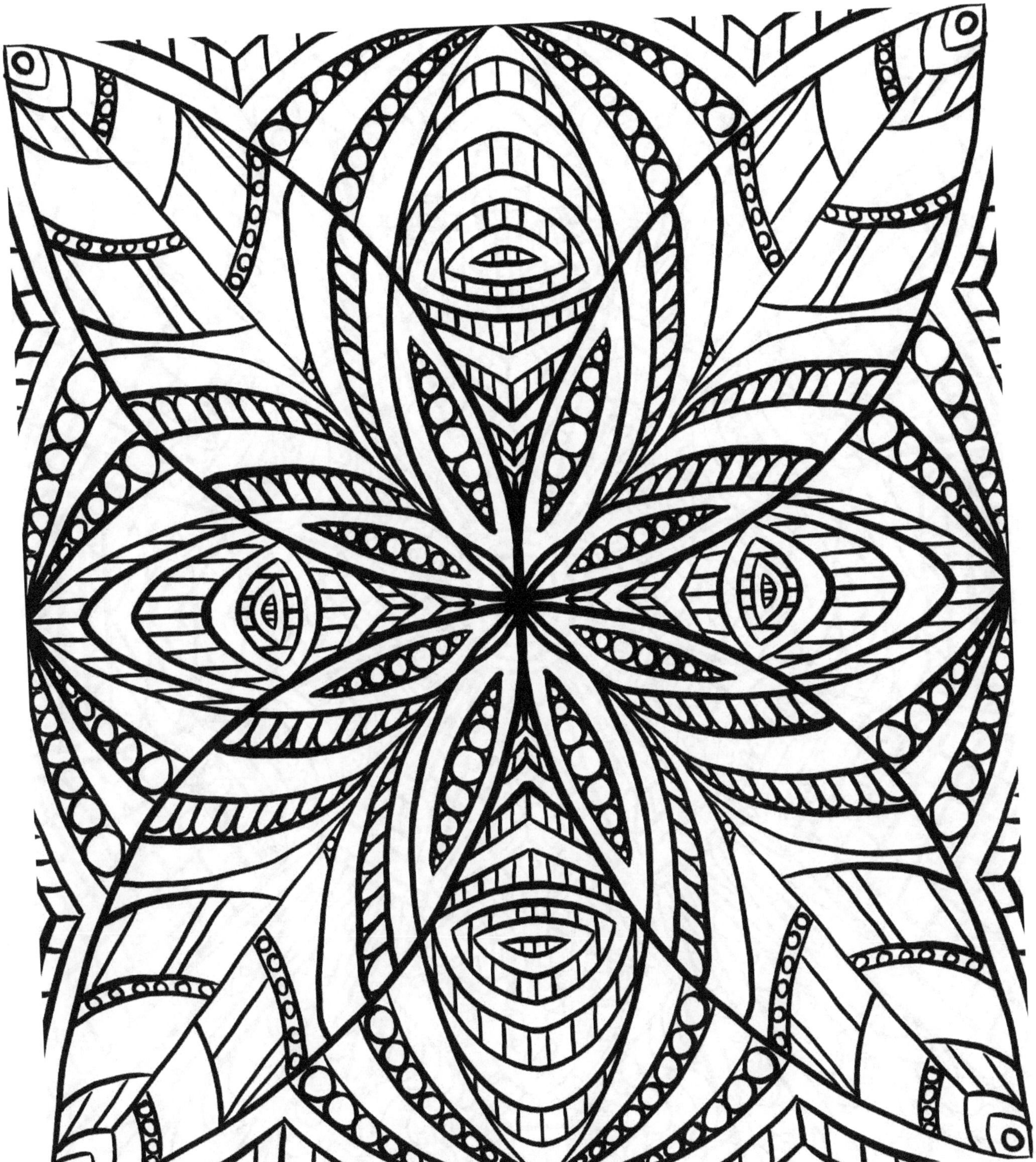

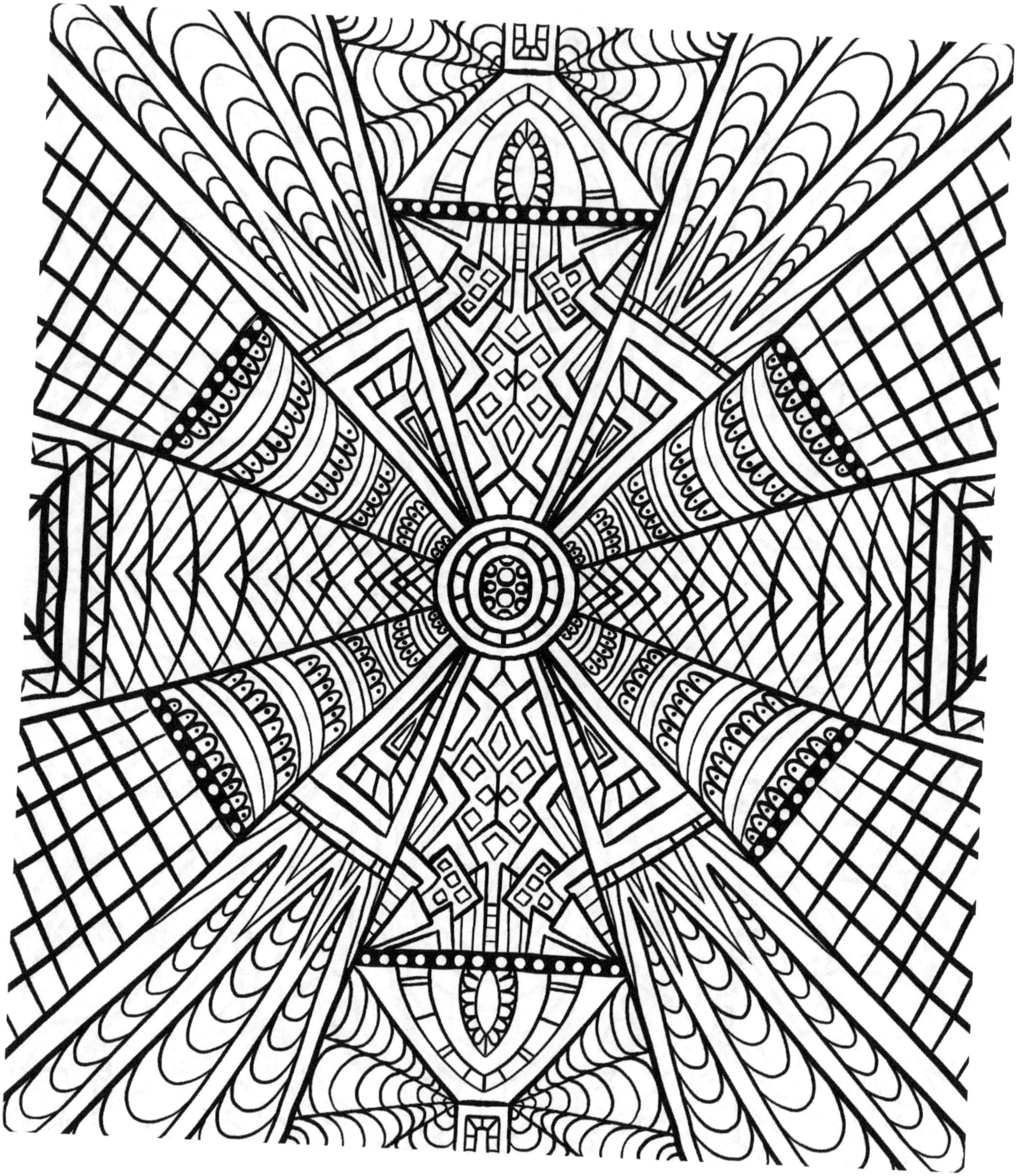

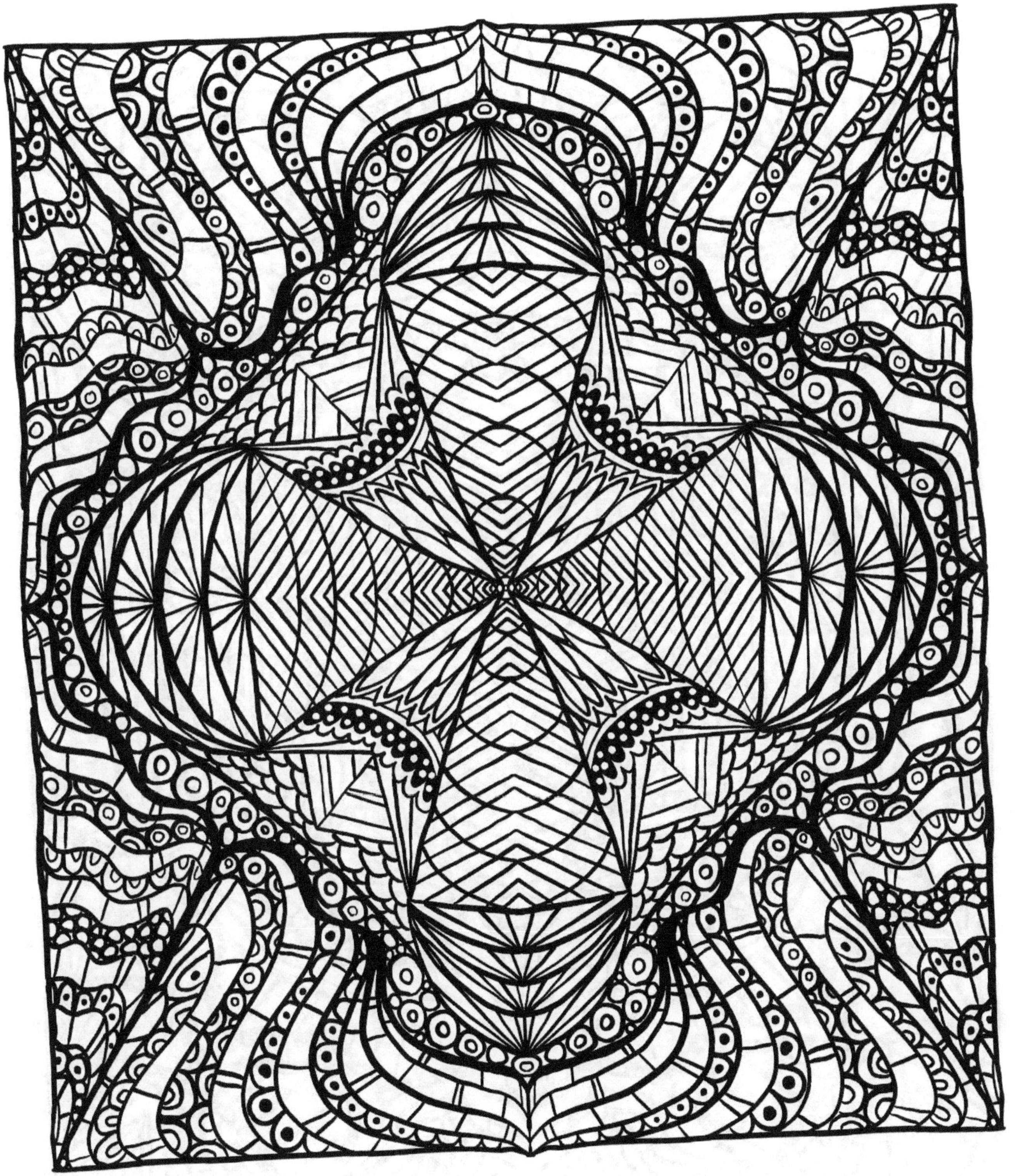

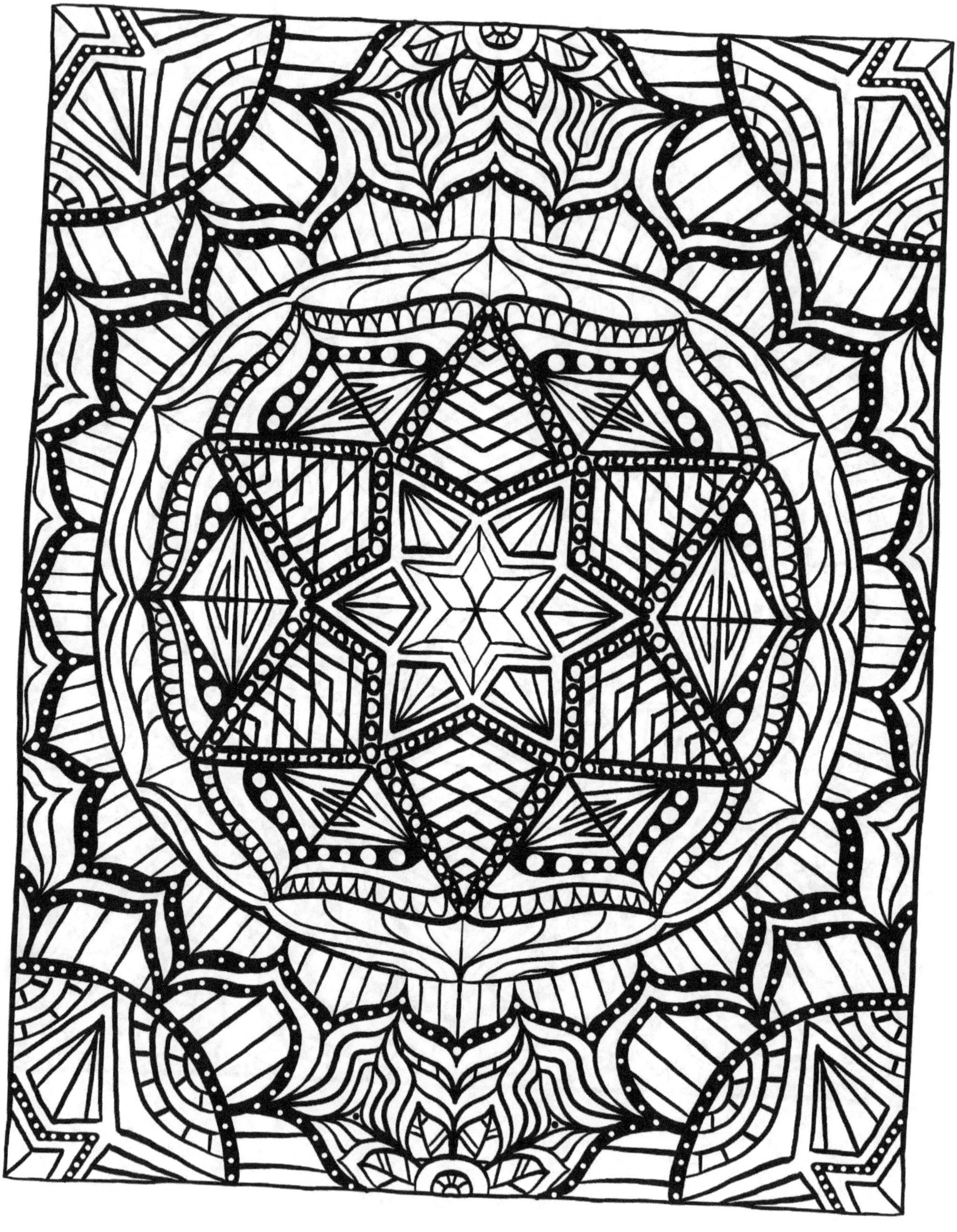

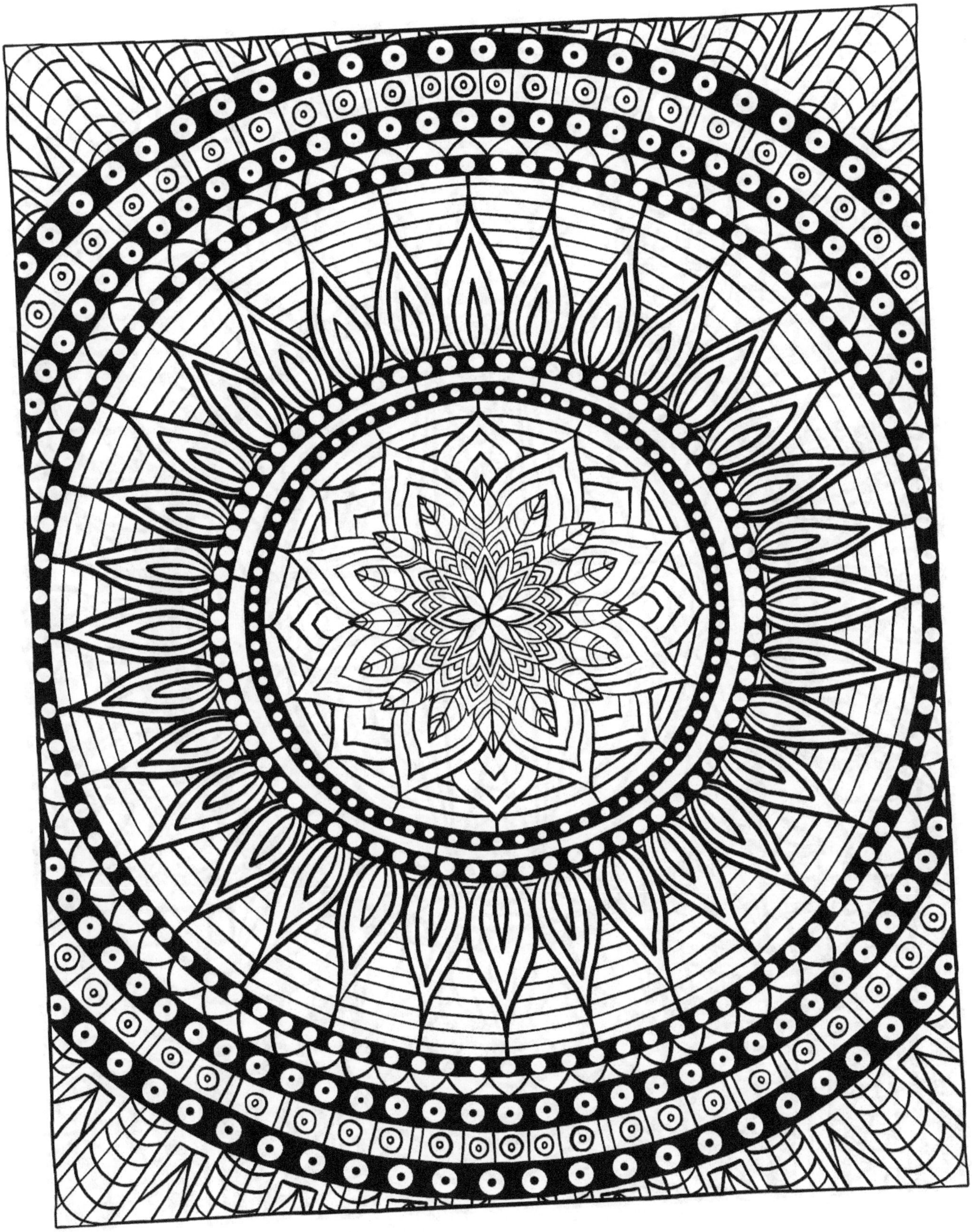

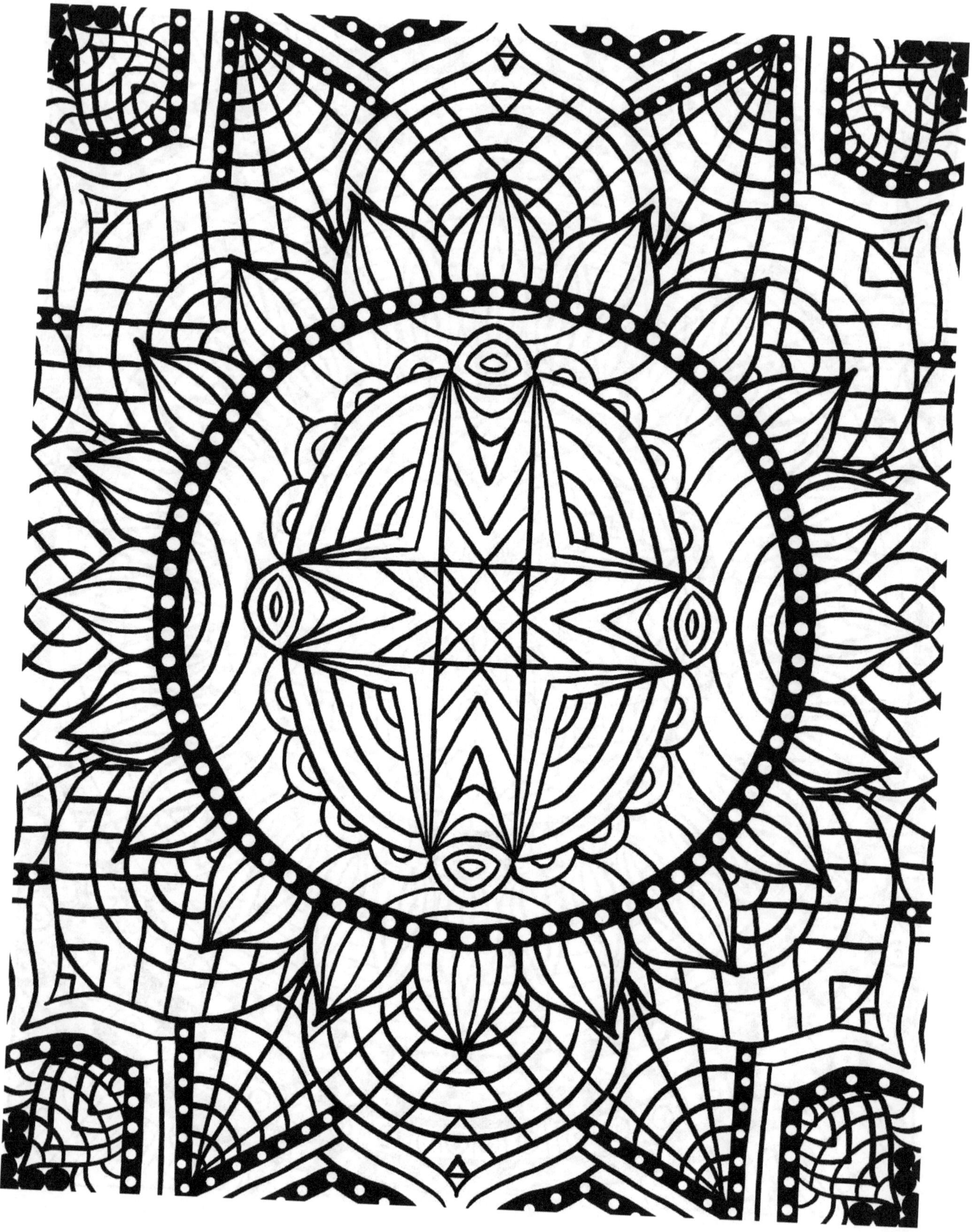

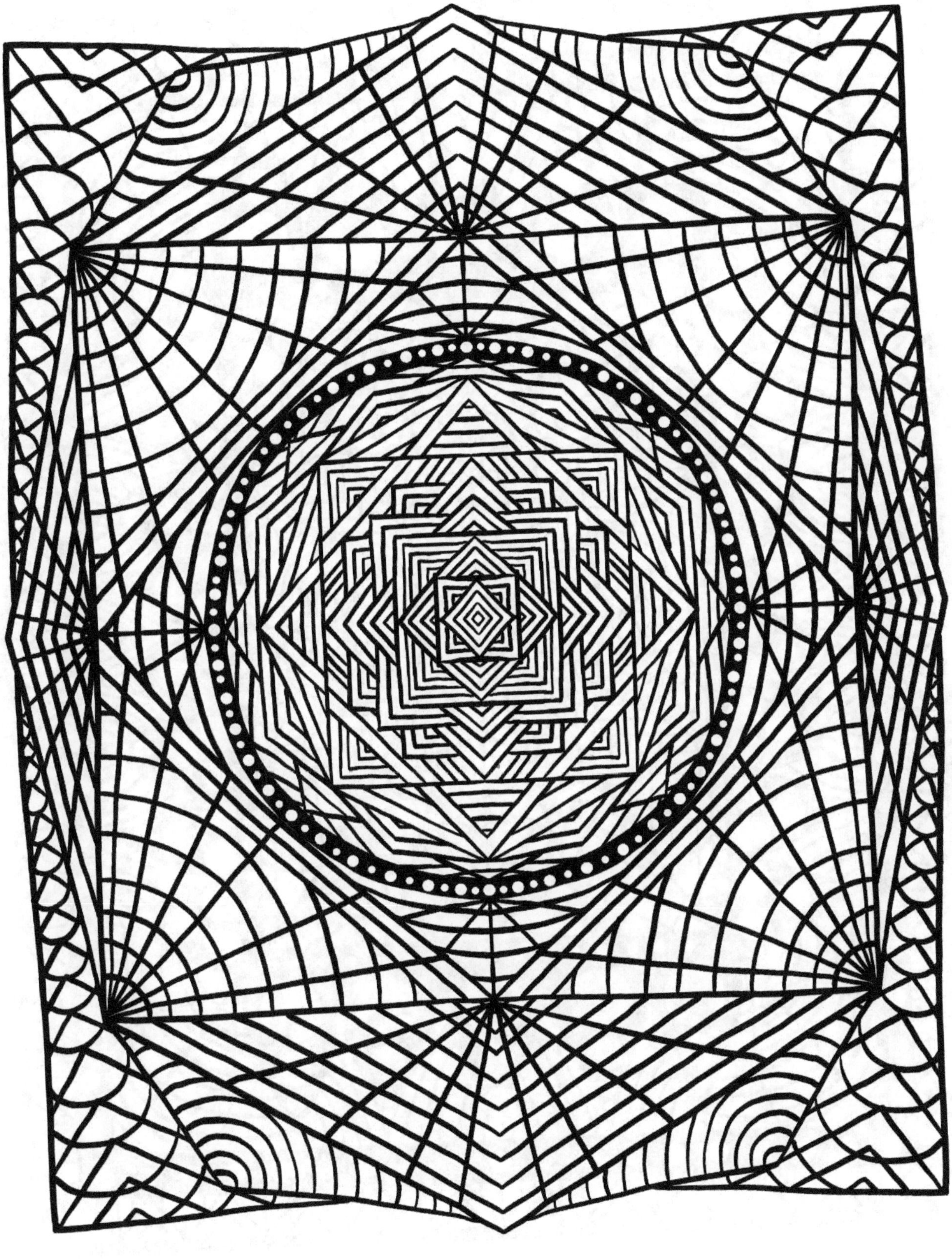

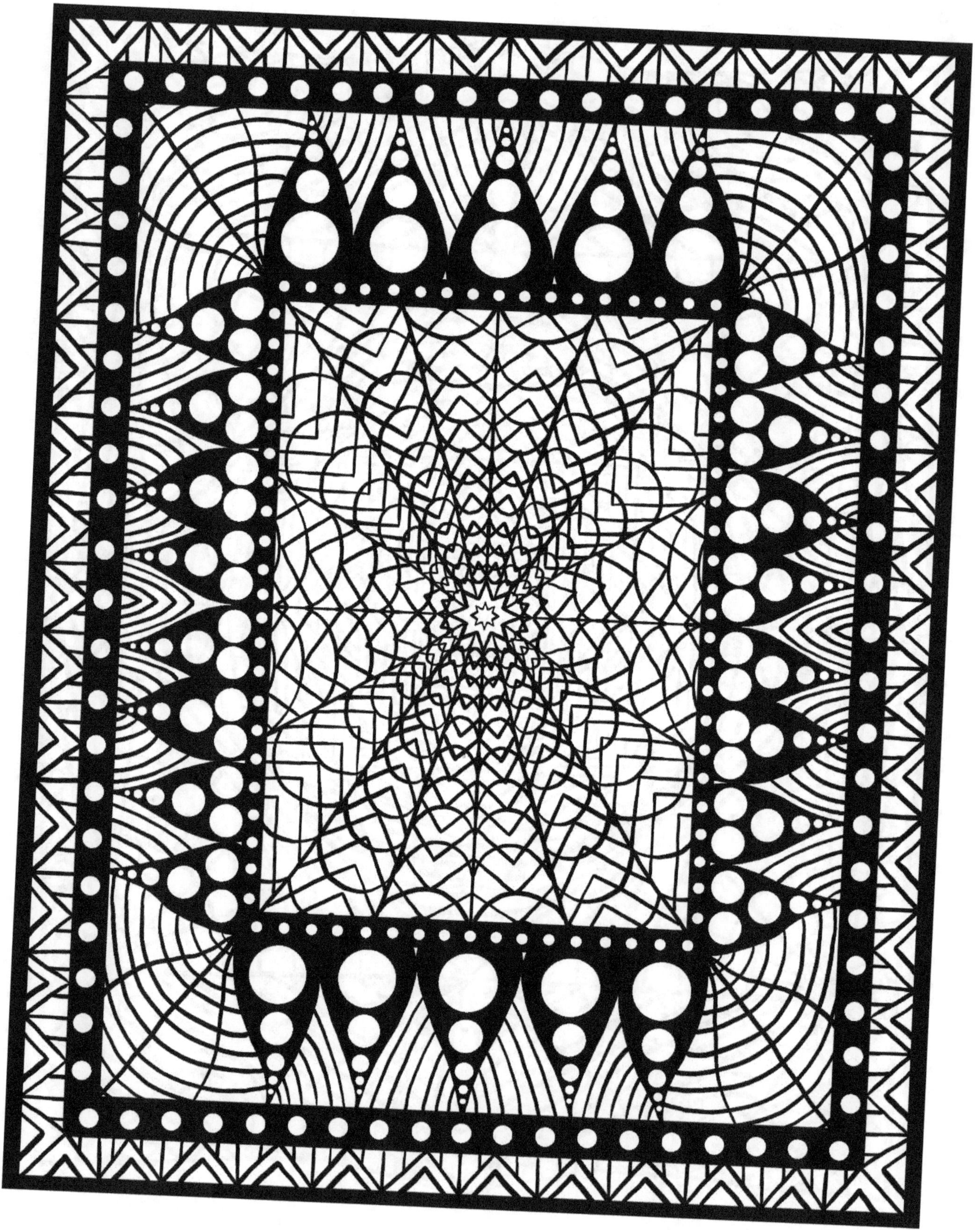

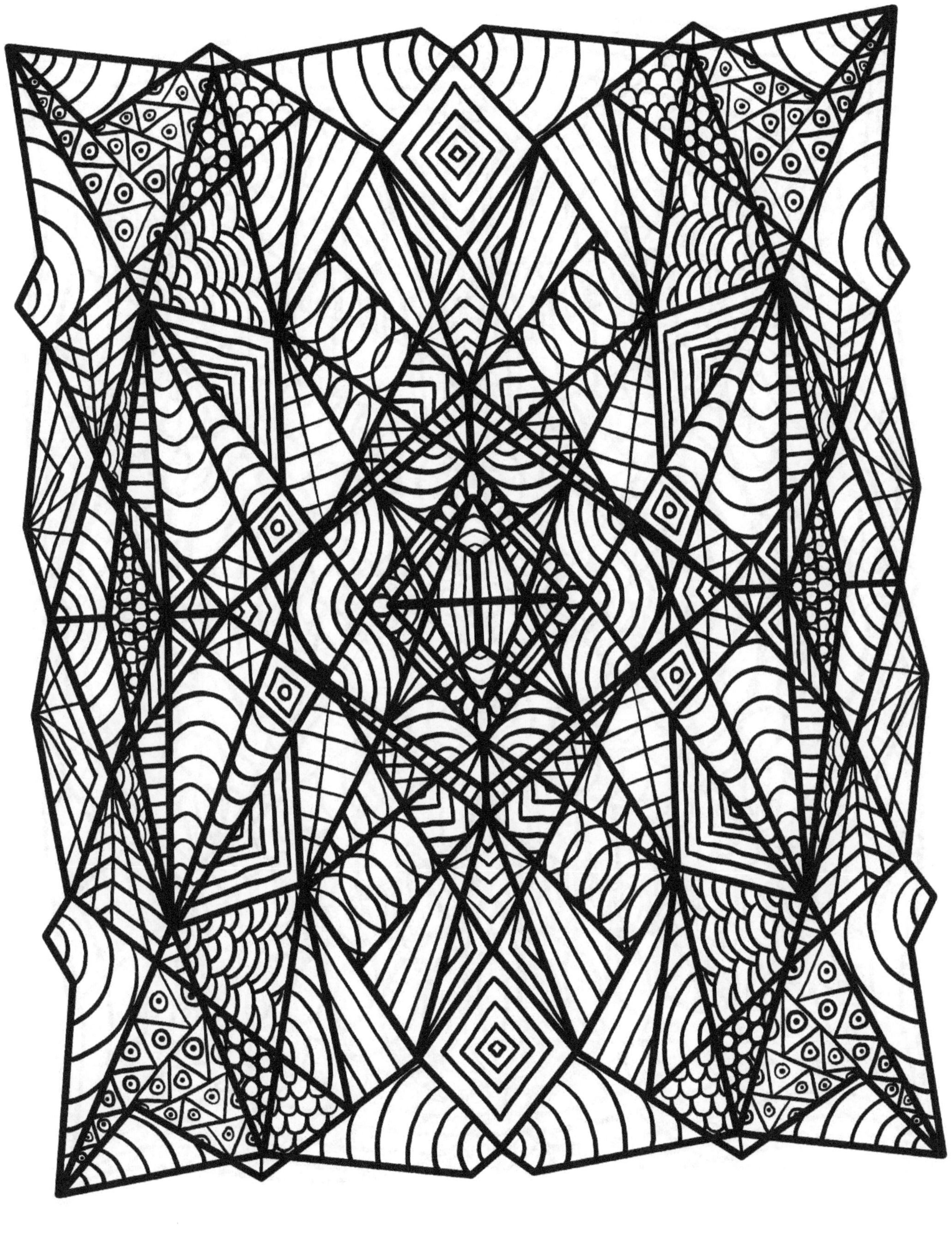

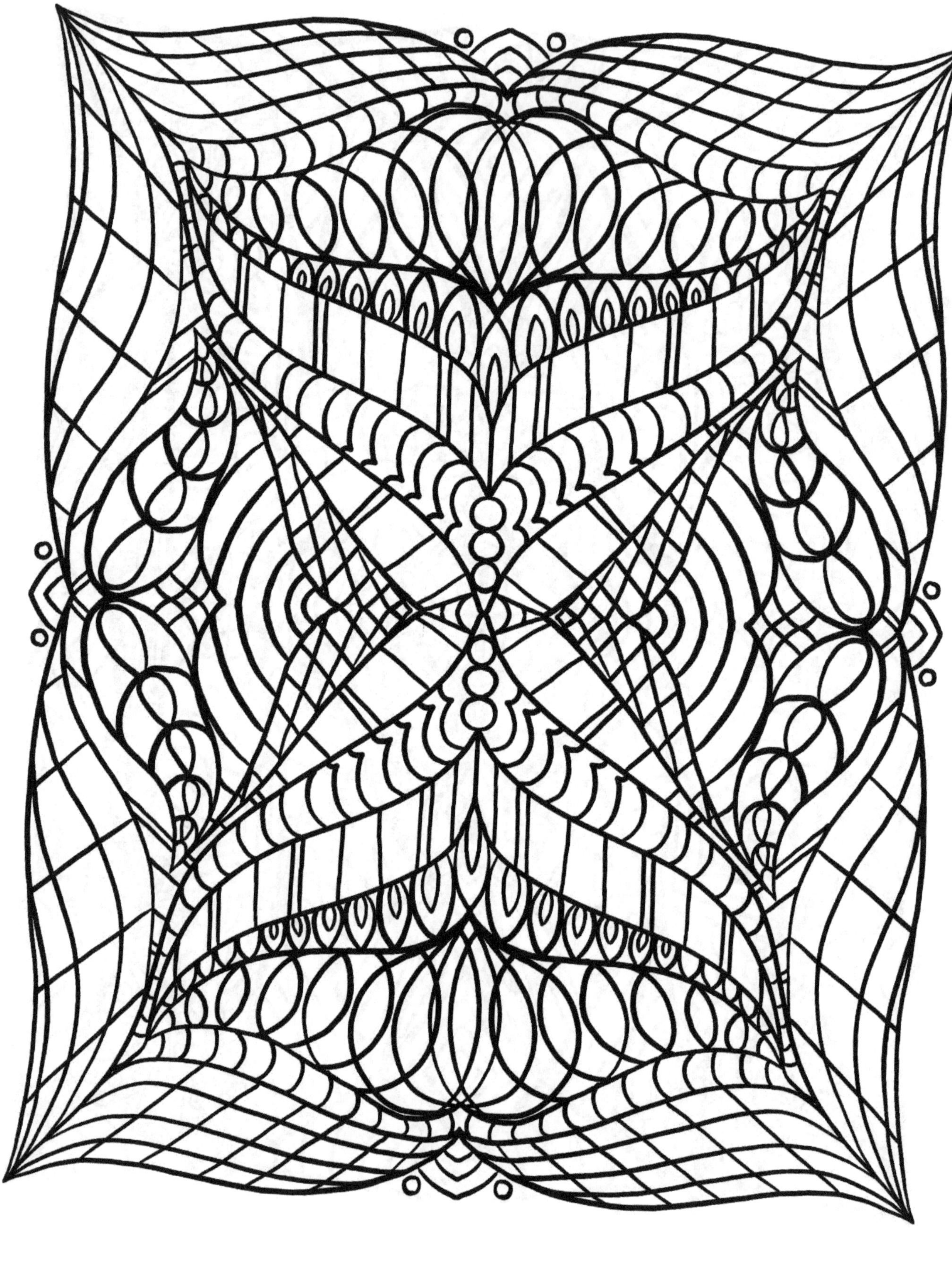

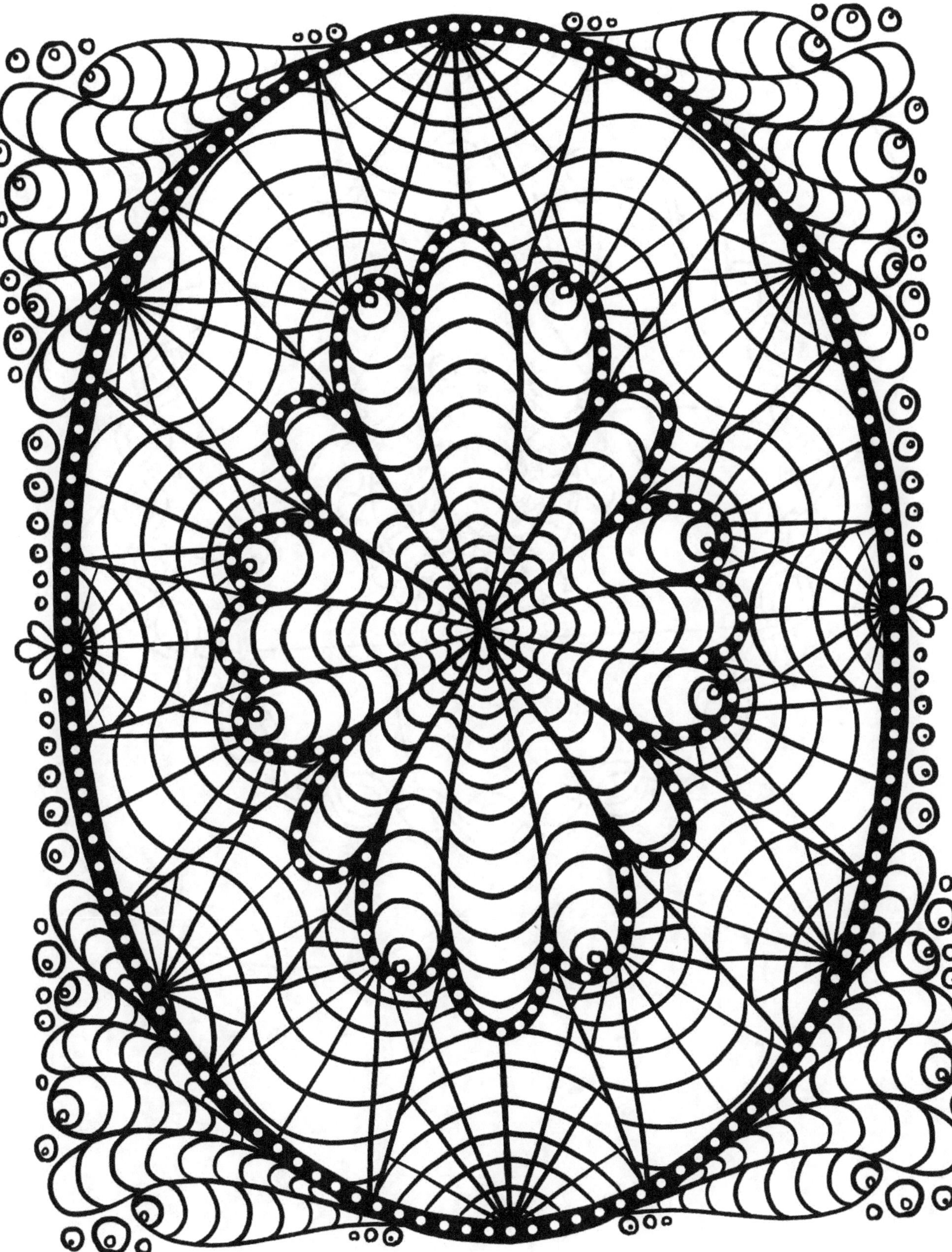

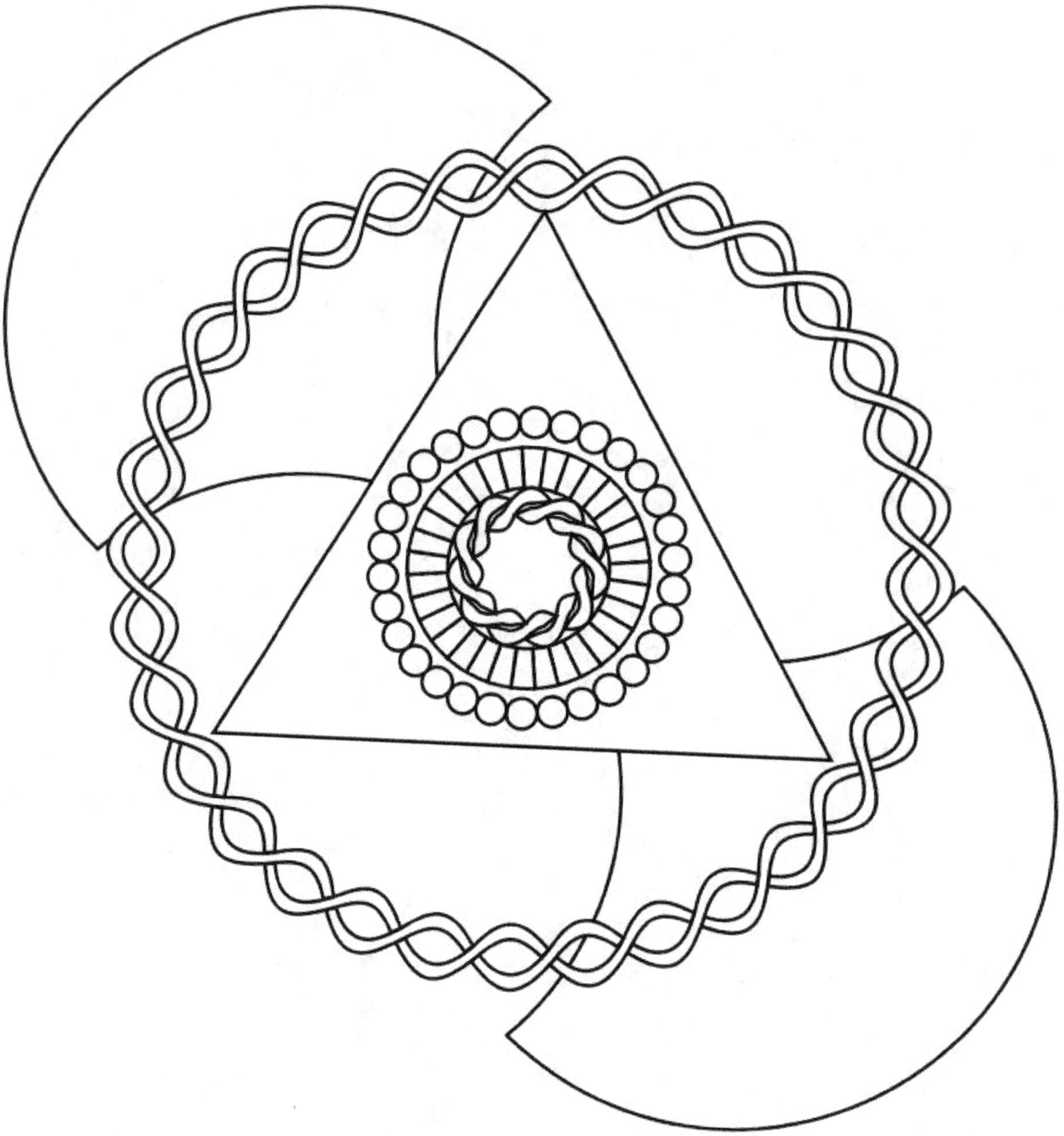

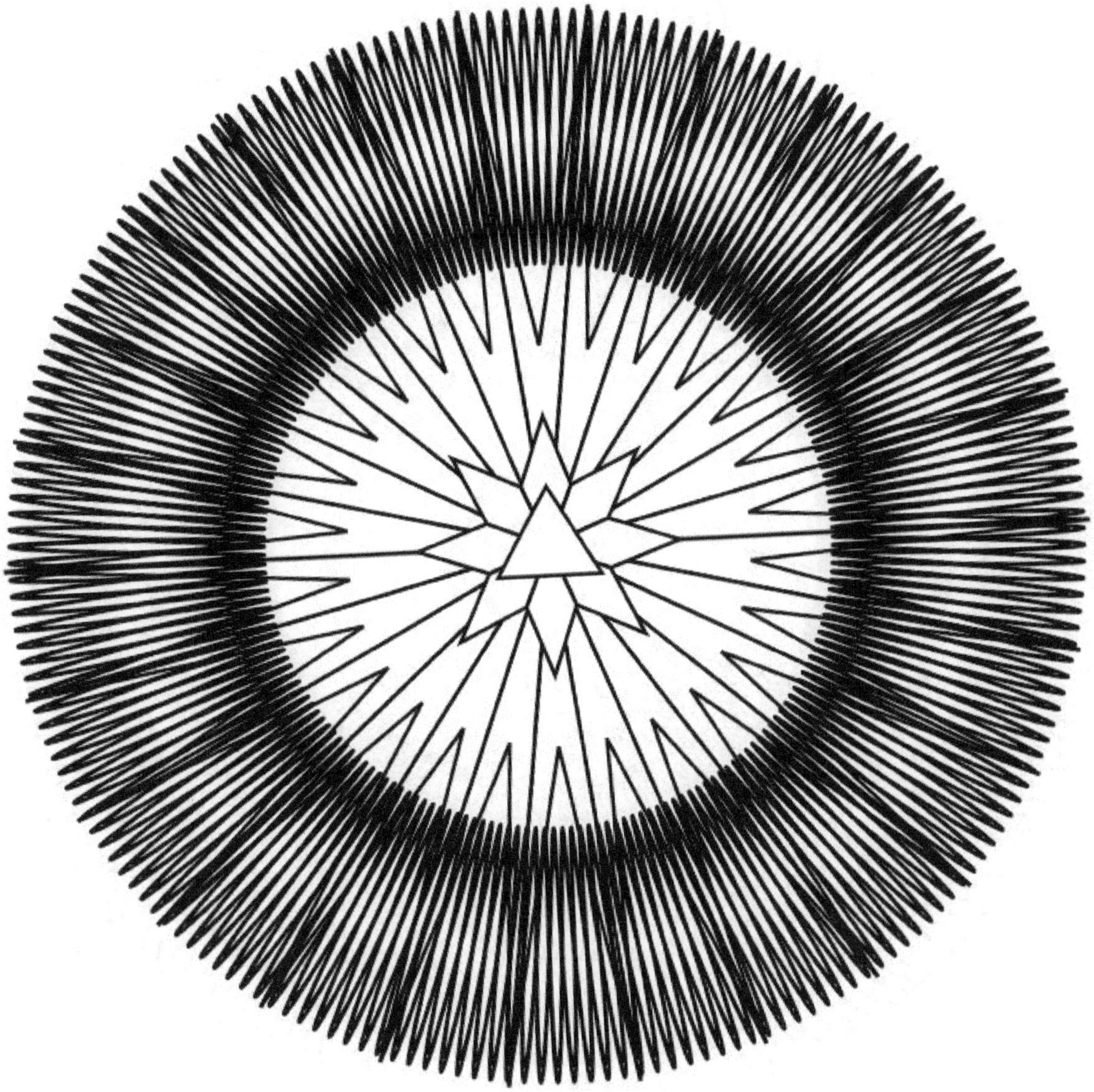

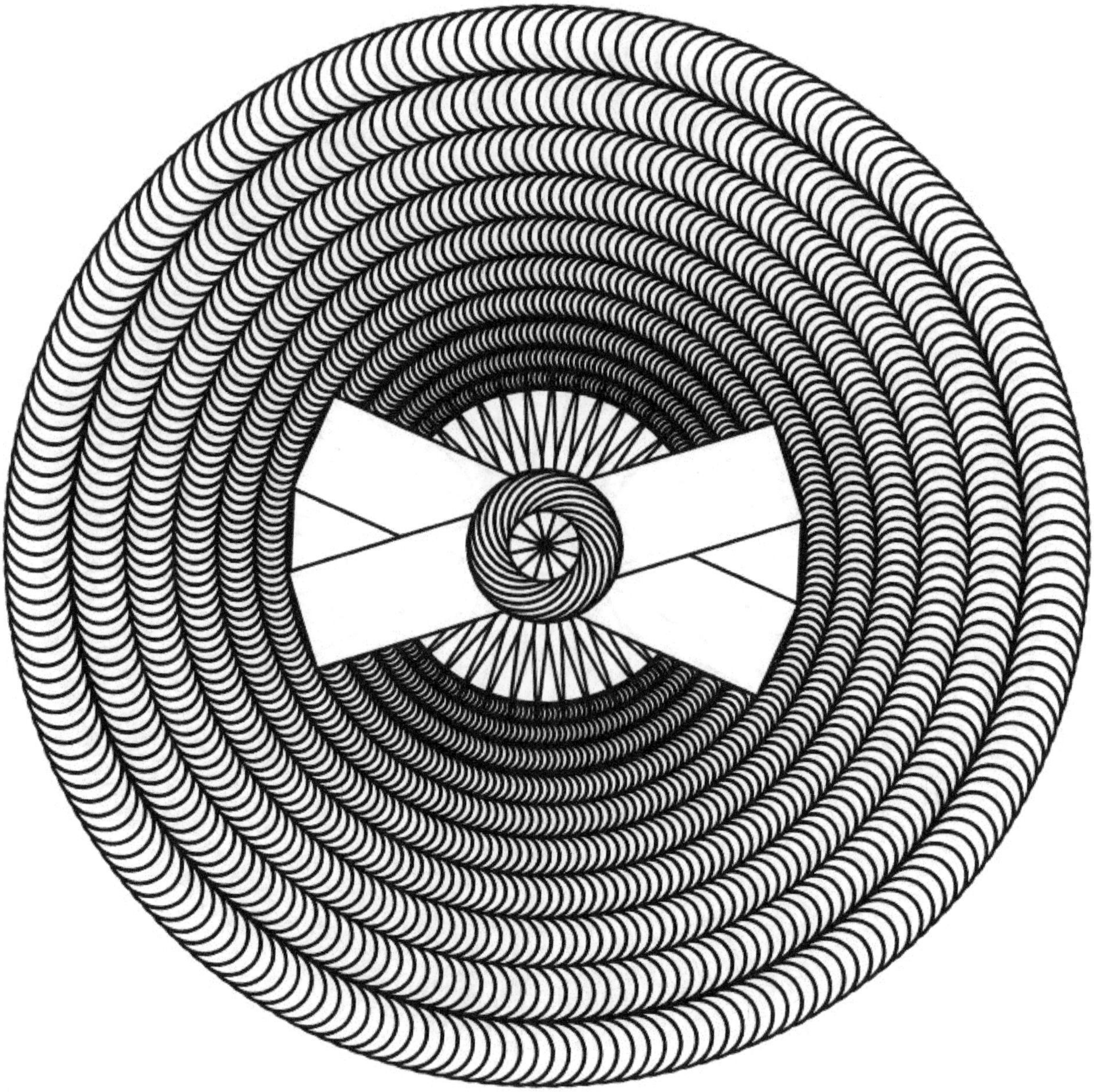

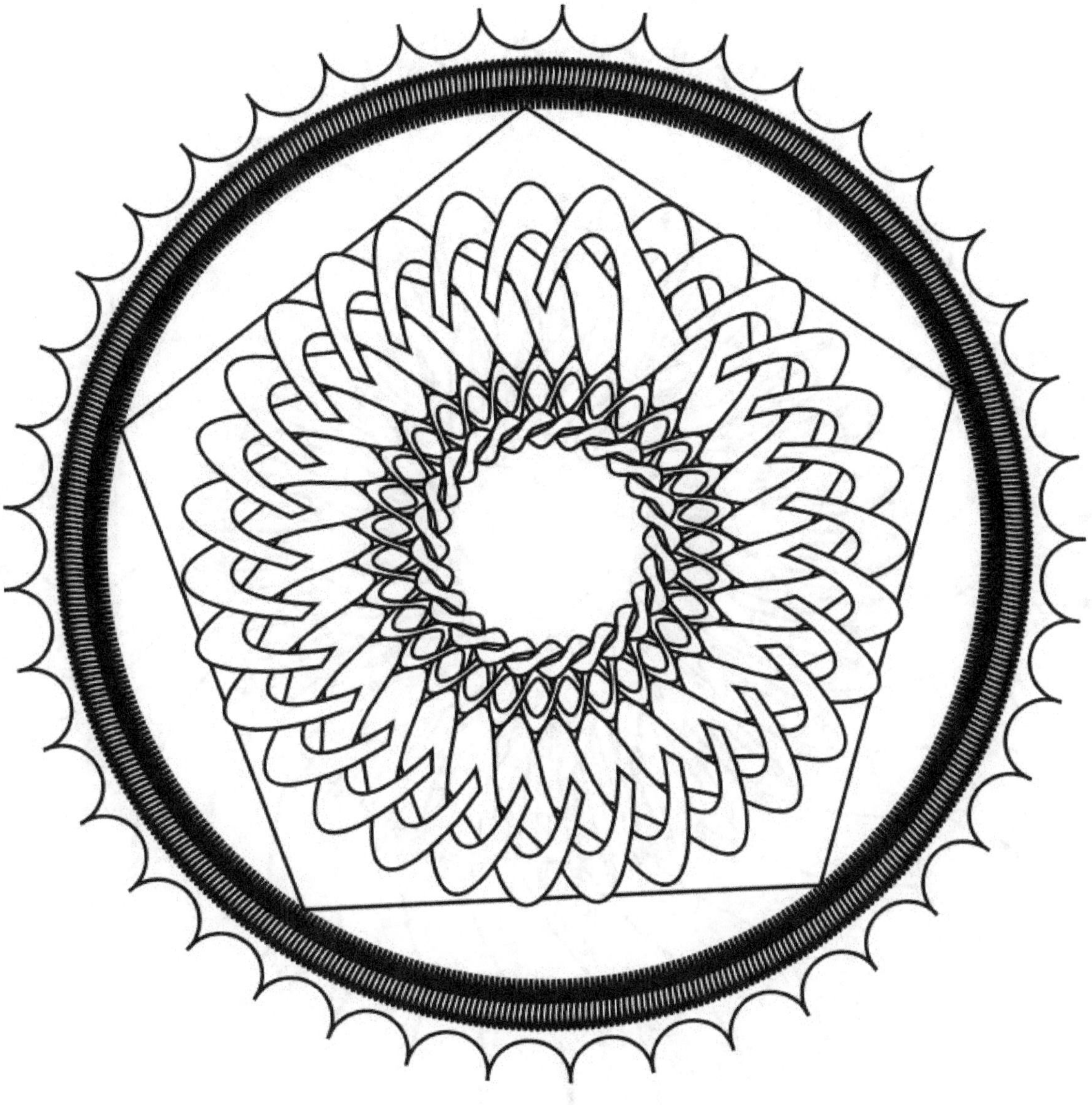

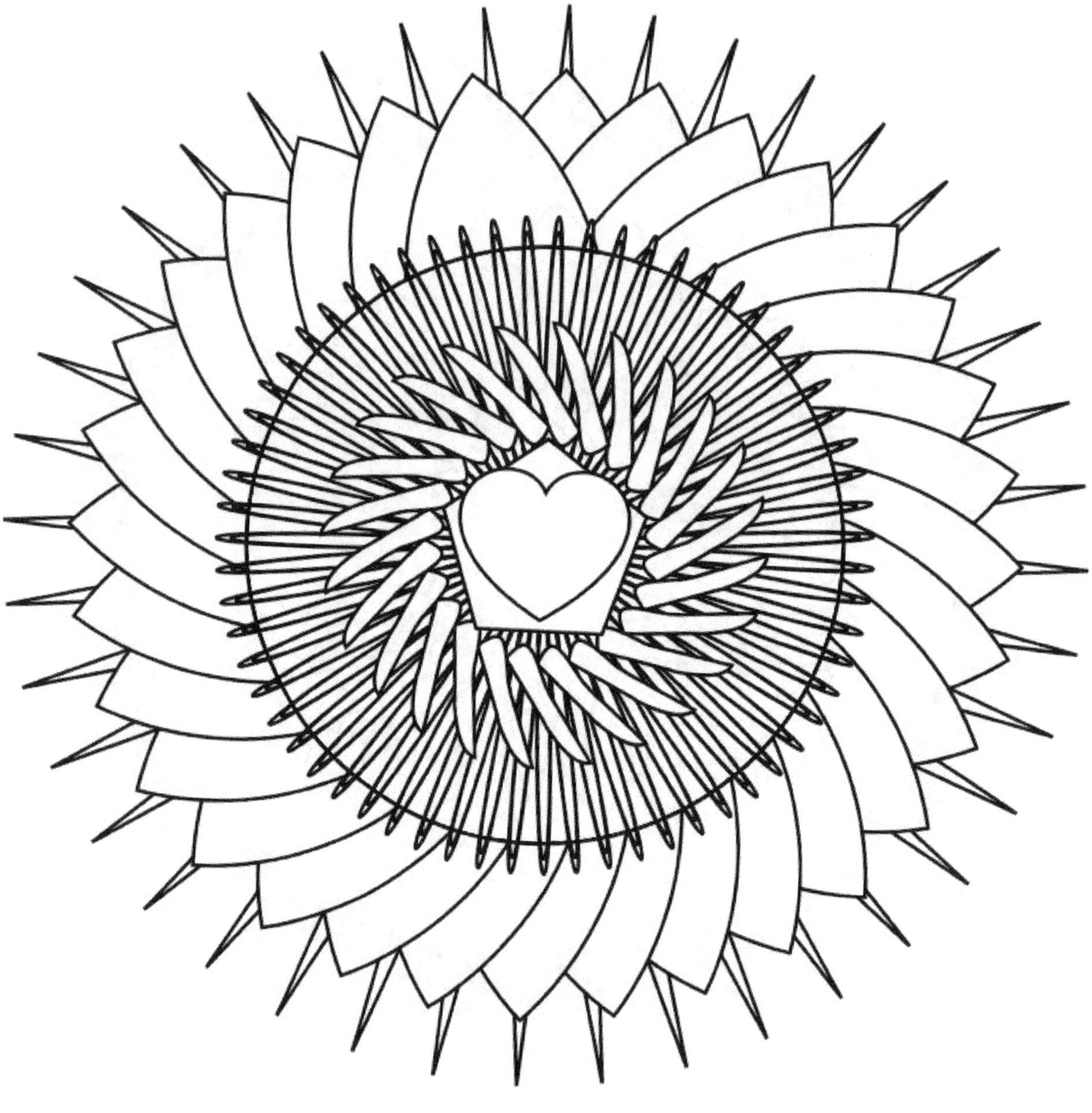

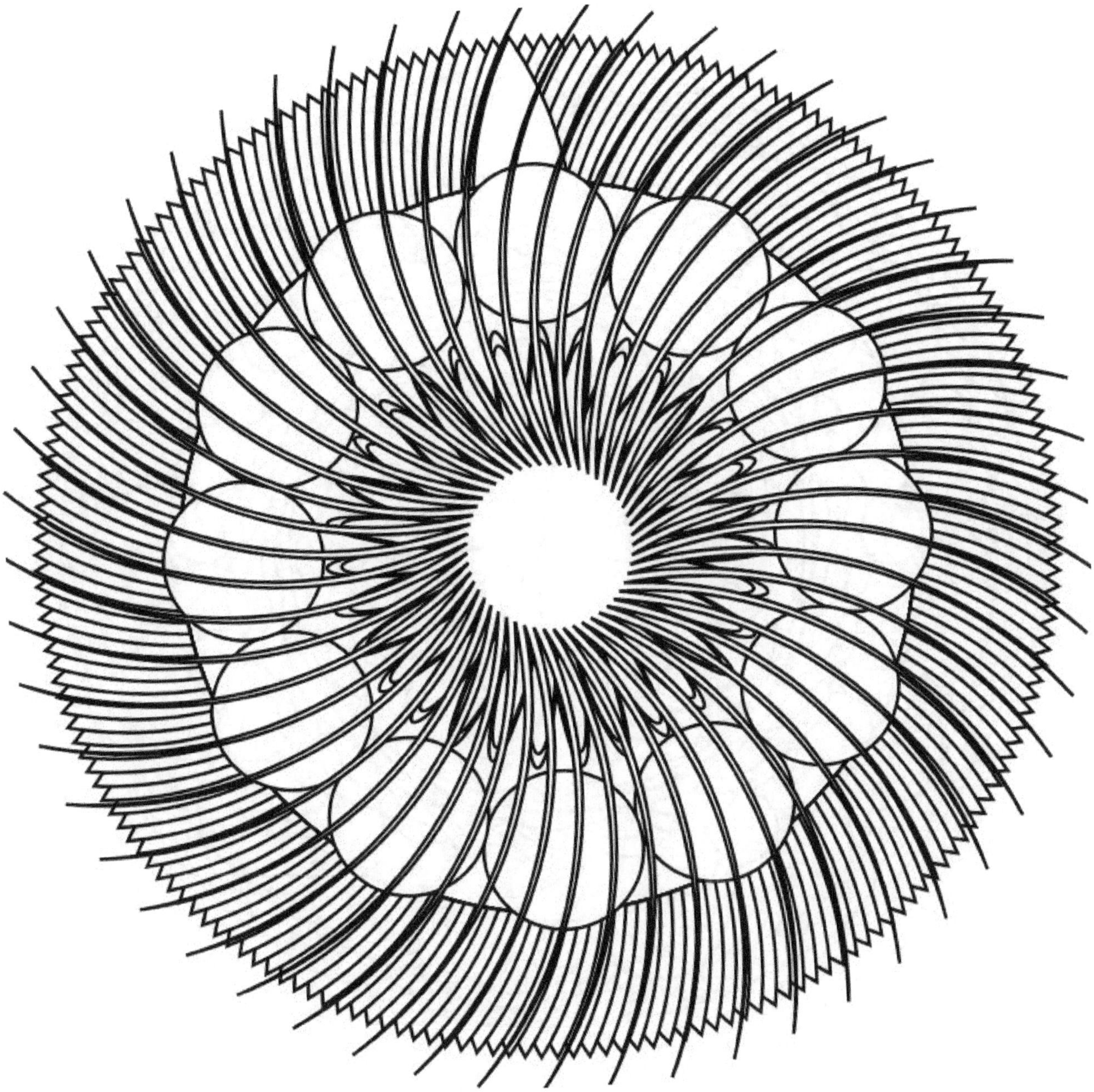

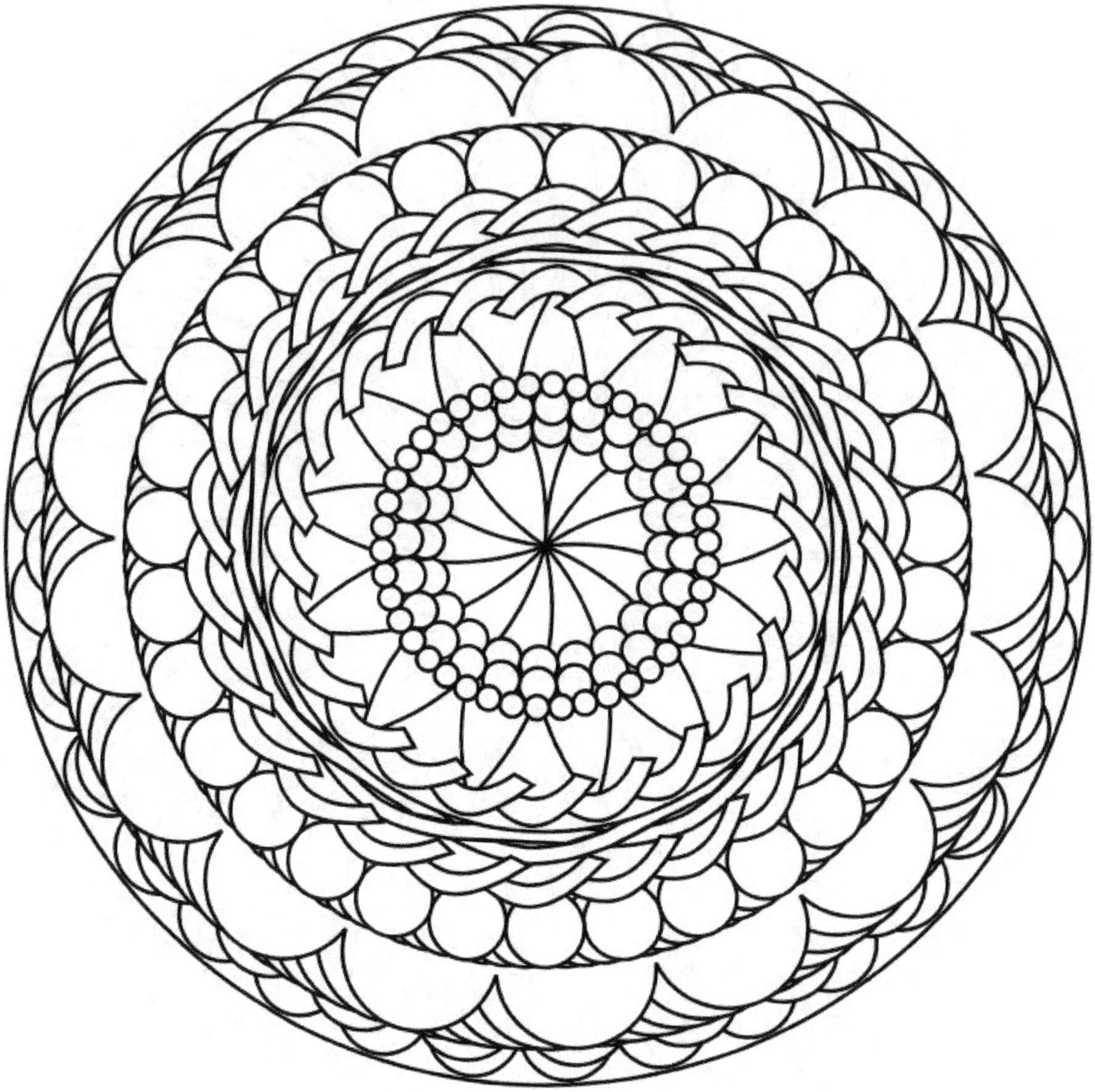

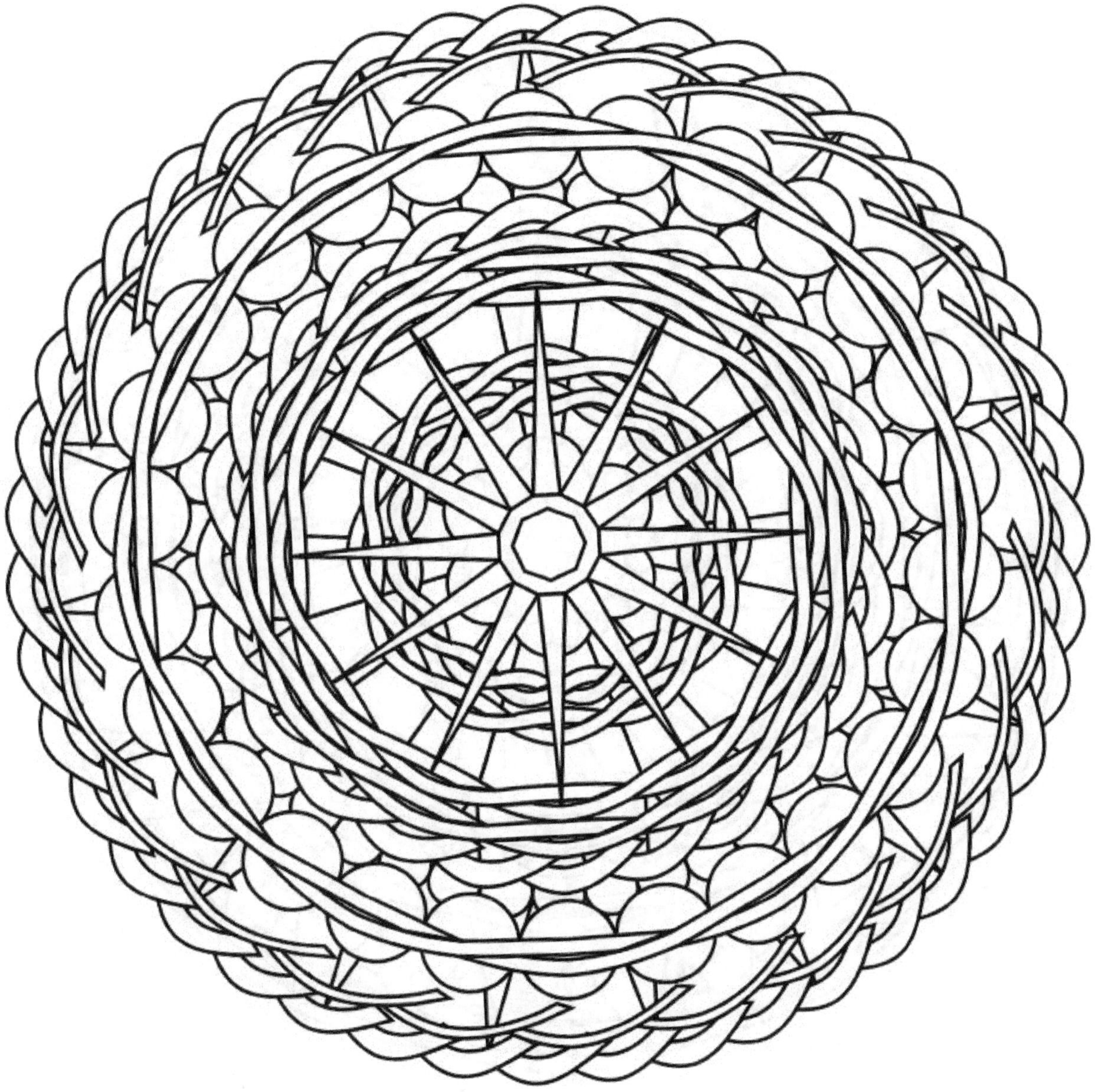

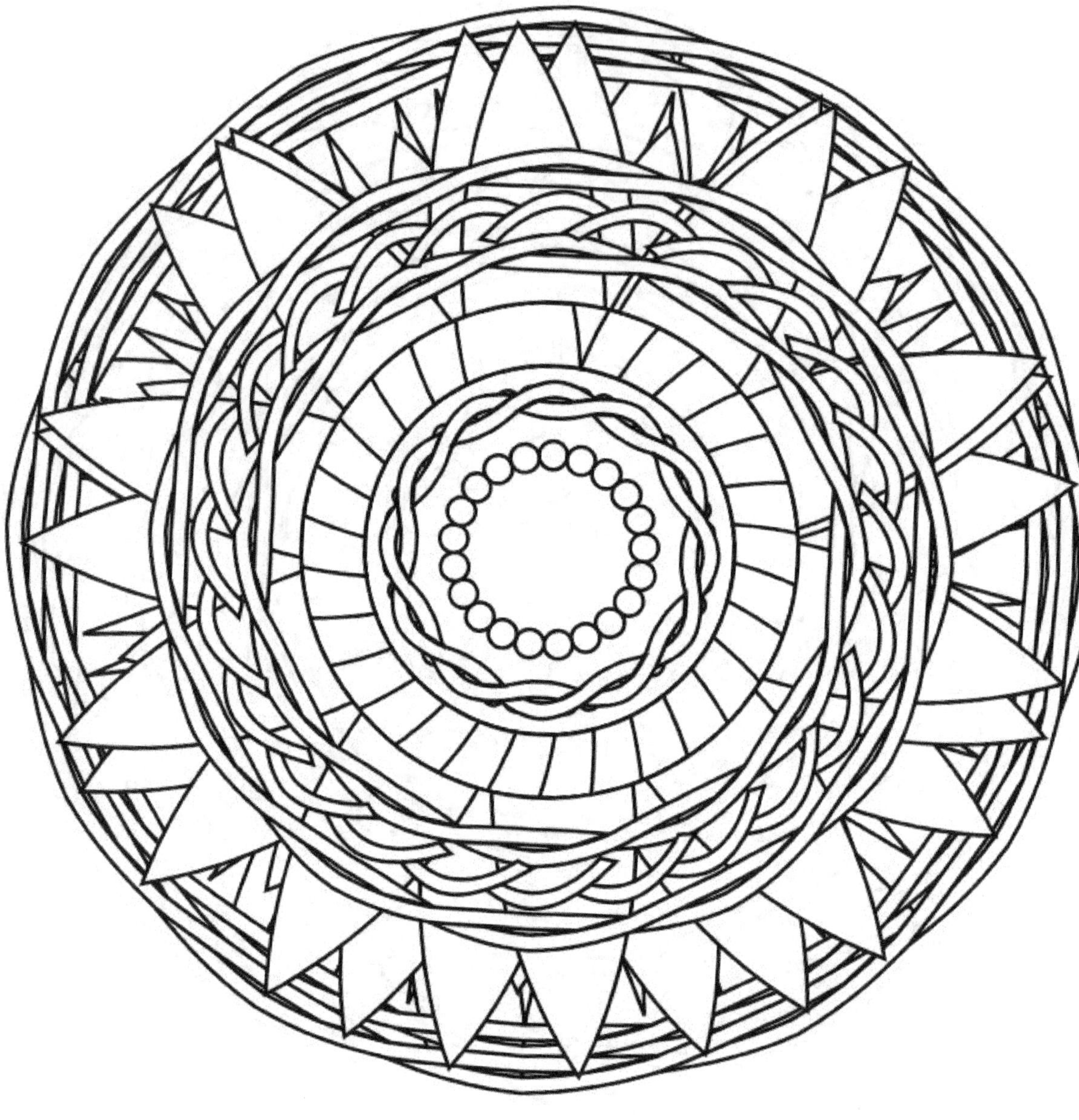

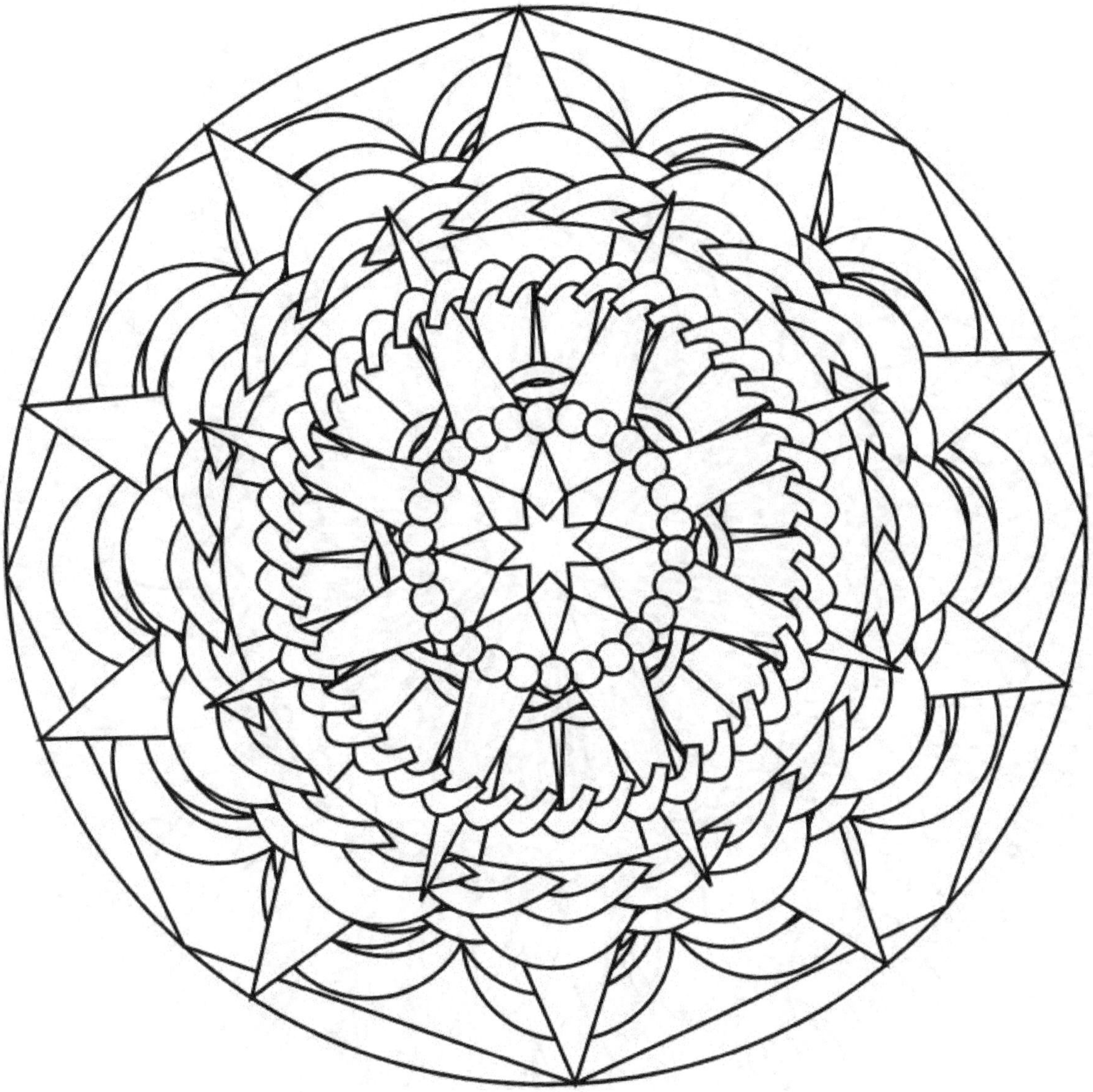

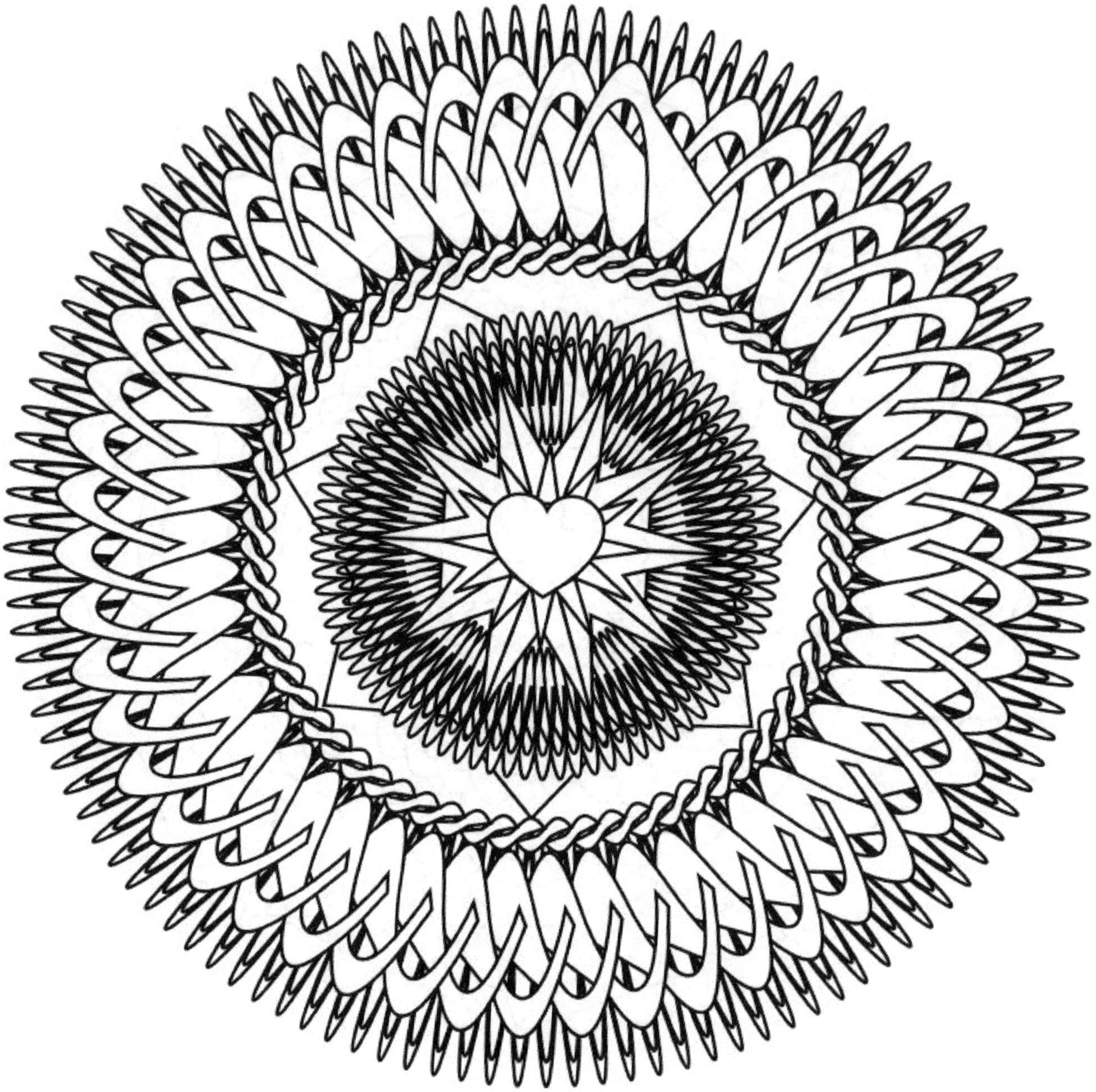

www.ingramcontent.com/pod-product-compliance
Lightning Source LLC
Chambersburg PA
CBHW080630180526
45168CB00007B/3115